THE HOPE PARADE

THE HOPE PARADE

Bringing Encouragement, Comfort, and Glorious Expectations Into Your Adversity

Roger R. Ziegler

Copyright © 2020 Roger R. Ziegler
All rights reserved. No part of this book may be reproduced or used in any manner without written permission of the copyright owner except for the use of quotations in a book review.
ISBN-13: 978-1656658678

To My Precious Children…My Treasure

I dedicate this to you, Shelby, Brooke, and Luke.
May your hope be brilliant and everlasting as you
continue your journey without your brother, our son.
Noah will be missed until we are reunited once again.
Leading up to that day, we grieve with hope.

You all have my love forever.

Table of Contents

INTRODUCTION ix
HOPE...*Isn't merely a glimmer; it's a dazzling parade.* 1
My Present Trouble 2
HOPE...*Delivers* 5
The Villain: Adversity 6
HOPE...*Rises* 11
HOPE...Has No Expiration Date 13
HOPE...*Reaches* 15
HOPE...*Soars* 16
HOPE...*Illuminates* 19
Bully 20
HOPE...*Persists* 25
Man In the Clouds 26
HOPE...*Pierces fear* 30
Dante 32
HOPE...*Is contagious* 41

HOPE...*Ignites* 42
In Sickness and In Health 43
HOPE...*Renews* 51
My Darkest Days 52
HOPE...*Is Jesus* 57

INTRODUCTION

There you are—standing at the threshold that leads to chaos, which is your oncoming threat. You stare motionless at a tremendous and towering ocean wave about to crash down upon your life. You stand frozen, paralyzed with fear. With little or no warning you realize the ominous pounding which is about to take place. Then, you take your deepest breath in preparation to be plunged beneath a deep ocean for a great length of time. Your eyes instinctively shut for protection and the immense thumping in your chest is your heart muscle now in overload.

This is a common reaction and these instincts are designed to protect us. But, without having a source of help intact, you are really helpless and rely solely upon the massive breath you stored in your lungs. That's right, your only hope...is air.

Suppose I told you that you could have an emergency kit strapped to your body during one of these episodes. Maybe in one of those tactical backpacks or something. It would contain a life jacket, a waterproof LED light source, air-tight goggles, diving fins, an oxygen tank with all of the gear AND a life raft. Would you want to know more? I thought so.

Because life comes at us sideways and in unexpected and unannounced ways, we must be prepared to handle these circumstances beforehand. The security of knowing you have such amazing tools for life's brutal smack-downs should deliver a certain measure of comfort. So that when adversity calls your number and rubs its diabolical hands together in preparation to bring misery to your life, you have an answer. You have an immovable lighthouse perched on high among stormy seas to guide and direct you. You have peace in advance knowing that no matter what happens you have security.

With that being said, let me introduce you to something so magnificent it requires your undivided attention. I call it—The Hope Parade—and it's coming to a trial near you.

Oh, you've never heard of such a thing? Let me explain further. Picture this: a larger-than-life procession of powerful inspiration. More fabulous than merely floats and with greater fanfare than a talented marching band, moving in sequence and in constant forward motion. Festive and dazzling to the eyes and hearts; a gala public display like a holiday parade on Main Street. Except, this parade doesn't march through the wonderful streets of bliss and happiness, of peace and safety. Oh, it can, but it's meant to enter the places where the hopeless ones reside.

Instead of a sunny paradise, this parade slowly advances through our desert struggles, within the blistering cold loneliness, inside the barren and forsaken fields of fear, and along with the emptiness of oppression. It soars into the hearts of the troubled and afflicted; to uplift and point to perfect, unending hope.

Come all and witness the deliverance God has made. In the valley of the darkest shadows, here enters...The Hope Parade.

HOPE...*Isn't merely a glimmer; it's a dazzling parade.*

With wild fanfare and dazzling wonder of a parade, hope enters into your most desperate hour and rescues you from fear.
How many times have you been desperate? And how many of your moments were captured by fear?

Roger R. Ziegler

My Present Trouble

I was weary from trudging through these barren fields, so I sat there on the moist, cold ground. I had stepped over active minefields, stumbled through knee-deep desert sands, and wandered across decaying fields that once thrived as living crops and beautiful meadows, for far too long. It was time for my rescue; it was time for something to capture my wounded existence.

My aching arms could barely wrap around this shivering body as the howling wind beat against me sideways. The skies above wore the gloomiest dread and hung there heavy upon my shoulders. No matter how far I traveled, I couldn't escape this suffering landscape. It felt as though I lived in a world of shadows. The kind that seems to be cast from death's presence. But still, I had my breath and I wasn't a corpse.

As I helplessly sat there, I couldn't help but examine my surroundings. The ground exhaled its cold breath, mixed with coarse sand, shards of knife-edged stones, and the foul odor of moldy sludge beneath me. Miles in every direction, my view was impaled by nothingness; a vast barren "dead scape" is all I could see. Surely, I felt alone and this present inability to rise above was exhausting.

Suddenly, I realized this dreadful journey represented my life within the current circumstances I contended with. All of life's standard-issue trials and turmoil; difficulties at work or home, health problems with me or my loved ones, oppression from all sides, loss of life within my borders or crisis episodes that are ongoing, and the rest of them we all know.

Still, I remained in a beaten and powerless state because I was convinced that my surroundings were my only reality. I glanced down at my chest, arms, and legs and I was amazed at a mass grouping of arrows from earlier attacks. They struck with precision and each one had plunged deep within my tissues. I was under attack in every sort of way imaginable.

Maybe if I remained here a rescue party would locate me. Rescue party? Really? There's not a living soul for years in all directions, so I felt. Then, without warning, I heard a thin shriek of wind followed by a loud *FUMP!* and piercing pain in my right ribs. I collapsed onto the ground, over onto my left side writhing in excruciating pain shooting from deep beneath my rib cage. I quickly looked down just above my waist and I saw a new arrow that found its target. I panicked and my eyes scanned around for any visible threat but to no avail. To avoid another attack, I quickly picked myself up and staggered to my left, in the opposite direction. My lungs felt punctured and there was a new heaviness in my strained legs. How much longer could I endure this madness?

Thunder began to rumble and roar to warn me of its presence. I stumbled through obstacles endlessly without direction or purpose. Finally, I stopped to try and catch my breath. The bitter chill cracked my leathery lips and my heavy breathing caused them to bleed. I stood there motionless, lifeless except for my heaving chest and drooping shoulders synchronized with each inhaled and exhaled breath. My mind continued to focus on every single atrocity that impaled my peace. But, there were too many and I was overwhelmed by fear.

Roger R. Ziegler

And then I heard a faint sound in the distance. The ongoing thunder and wind were prominent but yet couldn't drown out this new resonance. My heart fluttered quickly with excitement as I turned my head towards the probable source of my help. I squinted to sharpen my view because I couldn't believe my eyes. From across a nearby open field came something I never had expected. It was...a parade. A procession with sounds of joyful delight, buoyant colorful images, and the continuous fluttering of the movement headed directly to where I stood. Impossible.

Immediately, my attention was fixed solely on this mirage-like fantasy and it captivated my heart. I ignored the pain and discomfort in my limbs and lungs; the chaotic environment that once brainwashed my mind was interrupted by a new influence. As it neared steadily, I could hear what sounded like my name being celebrated and heard encouraging cheers. My spirit was lifted and I felt a new strength infused within me. The brilliant light beaming from around this parade illuminated my surroundings. What was once a nightmare-like landscape was now overlaid with a brightness that looked like a sheer, alternate scene. A field of decayed trees now appeared healthy and vibrant, yet I could still see their former dead condition beneath this bright layer. I was given a new vision. This was so bizarre in the most sensational sort of way!

Suddenly, I felt a tremendous dose of pure hope fill every part of me. The kind that is not superficial or brief, but hope that sustains, breathes life and carries broken hearts through every sort of trouble. I was revived and gained new confidence. I could continue on through my trials and my adversity, but with a fierce and unwavering glorious expectation.

At the center of all of this surprising and wonderful expectation was Jesus Christ, the Prince of Peace. Together we will travel through the storms of life and He will be my ever-present comfort. It is through His living, loving eyes that I will see. And it is because of His presence I am rescued. Delivered through His provision, by His love...The Hope Parade He sent just for me.

HOPE...*Delivers*

Sometimes a heart-shaped rock appears during a walk through the woods and I'm reminded of the hope that I have. In those simple yet effective reminders, God chooses to display a wink to let us know He's there. In the most unexpected moments, He comforts us.
God's love caresses and is nurturing. Through it, He delivers peaceful security. He never sleeps or forgets us and considers each one of us to be the apple of his eye. With the very essence of God's nature, He is my everlasting hope.

Roger R. Ziegler

The Villain: Adversity

Ladies and gentlemen, allow me to introduce you to someone you are probably already quite familiar with. In fact, you just might be life-long acquaintances. An entity that goes by many names and aliases; a character both sinister and devious. So, without further ado, I present to you...adversity.

Well, did you expect someone else? Perhaps a celebrity, a famous Nobel Peace Prize recipient, or a world-renown surgeon? Sorry to disappoint you. But please, make yourself comfortable as I delve into a more thorough description of this fiend.

Adversity is like a raging rhinoceros that suddenly crashes through the doors of a tidy and pristine boutique. An exquisite storefront with displays of priceless glass ornaments, beautiful porcelain figurines, and elegant dinnerware. *Oh my*, you exclaim, is right! You can imagine the chaos immediately infused within this most peaceful and serene setting, now abruptly turned upside down.

The Hope Parade

At least fifteen-hundred-thousand-million fragments exploding similar to fairy dust in a Peter Pan motion picture. And the behemoth rhino nowhere in sight, but a trail of said particles that remain as evidence of a quick four-legged escape made through an exit wound of drywall and ornately designed wallpaper. A disaster is an understatement, but that is exactly what we now have.

So, I hope you embrace my example and understand what we all are dealing with. *All*, you ask? Yeah. We all encounter adversity in an assortment of terrible ways. From the moment we are born until the very moment we breathe our last, this villain is certain to wreak its best havoc on our collective lives.

And consider this chilling thought: adversity took a number and it is waiting patiently in line until it is called to enter everyone's life. For some, it's a terrible migraine headache that sidelines your best day; for others, it's an unexpected car wreck and a calendar filled with expensive medical appointments that follow; and for some, it's a life-threatening illness that throws jabs and punches every hour of every day—it's unmerciful. No matter the trial, ugly circumstance, or human tragedy, the adverse situation will most definitely appear in our lives. The punch line is this–we don't know when or what it will look like.

Jesus said it this way in john 16:33:

"I have told you all this so that you may have peace in me. Here on earth, you will have many trials and sorrows. But take heart, because I have overcome the world."

I love how He told us so that we may have peace in Him. Not peace in our own supposed sufficiency, or in our ability to create a safe-haven that can provide security from disaster. No, He said we may have peace in Him. What an amazing statement! Jesus is our peace and sometimes in our course of life, we completely miss or overlook this fact.

Our human framework all too often relies upon our own ability which can navigate our hearts away from depending on Him for that peace, that security, and that assurance. Jesus said we can have peace in Him. So why do we go around Him in search of it?

Maybe we don't truly believe that Jesus is our peace when we give Him dominion over our lives. Maybe we strongly believe and on hold on to the grip that this world, this life had on us. Before we surrendered to his Majesty for salvation, we were caught in a web, like a prisoner in chains, and so distracted by our surroundings–our day to day existence. But because of God's grace and mercy, we were rescued from despair and from the choke-hold life once strangled us with.

Think about it, each day you probably woke up gasping for air— figuratively speaking (I hope)—and felt the mounting pressure begin to weigh you down. I mean right out the gate as you slipped off of your comfy mattress and pressed your feet onto the cold floor, you muttered with disdain, "Here I go again." Right? The same crud, different day. The rut of just surviving, but not thriving.

Then salvation called your name and you came running. The blinders were removed and the chains of despair were destroyed by Jesus. From that moment on you wore the banner of his victory upon your life and you could now face the day with a terrific boldness because of His love for you.

The days were brighter; the sun spread its warmth over you deeper; the perspective of life allowed for hope to suddenly appear in each new day. You jumped off of your bed with an opportunity to live in victorious fashion, because of His love. You took your day's first steps with a sense of upbeat charisma, because of His love. You found God's purpose in the hours ahead and a drive with meaning because of His love. There was nothing or no one who could stop His powerful love for you. Thank you, Romans 8:31, for reminding us of this powerful truth!

Then, adversity called your number…and you crashed. The realities of this life sucker punched you and you crumbled. Now what?

Remember, we don't know when or what adversity will look like, but most certainly adversity is on time. Just like clockwork. And it knows exactly what your life consists of. It knows your daily routine, it hears you utter your own fears, it understands your weaknesses, and it even knows your knee-jerk reactions to some of its best ploys to steal your joy.

Yeah, this monster is slick and diabolical for sure. With malicious intent, affliction waits patiently to unleash some sort of pain and measure of suffering upon you. Hardship breathes by your distress and feeds upon your fear.

Want to hear the good news? Of course, you do. Well, adversity is always on time and is allowed into our lives, but is kept on a leash. That's right—a leash. Like a rabid wild dog. A leash that restricts, limits its touch, regulates its power and controls its effect upon our lives. Don't believe me? Read the story of Job in the Bible.

The beginning of this amazing story tells us that Job was a God-fearing, blameless man and that he stayed away from evil. He lived with integrity and had God's favor upon him. Then we see the adversary, the devil, the accuser, and he was looking for someone to pounce on, like a hungry lion. Then, God did something that blows my mind. He offered Job to be persecuted; places him directly into the hands of the enemy. But, and this is huge, but He limits the devil with specific restrictions—hence the leash. At this point in chapter one, God only allows the master of disaster open reign upon Job's family and his possessions—not Job physically.

The point I'm making here is that the villain was allowed by the hero only limited affliction to the victim. Satan was given specific orders by God who was in control of Job's situation completely. Now don't lose heart in chapter one. Please, I ask that you read the entire book all the way through and explore God's truth in his living word. Yes, even though Job was stricken in so many ways—his children died, his possessions destroyed and taken, and his own body crushed with illness—yet he remained faithful to the Lord and stayed the course of obedience.

Job is made of the same fabric and spirit we all are. You see, undoubtedly his life is consecrated to the majesty and presence God had in his life. Job made a decision to serve the true and living God; to live with integrity and walk humbly with Him; to remain faithful to God in the face of danger and ultimate destruction; to remain hopeful as the waters of calamity rose to life-threatening levels, and Job had the most powerful hope that could ever be possessed in anyone's life—the hope of God. Is there really any other?

The same God who reigned in Job's life is the same God who reigns in our lives today. Remember that God willingly placed Job in harm's way, not as a sadistic means, but rather He knew and believed in Job.

God lovingly looks upon us and cheers for us every time we're at bat, have the football, put on that uniform, go to work or school each day, or step into a new adventure with opportunity for us to shine powerfully. It may not look like that from our standpoint, but be assured—God believes in you. Wait, you may have been taking a bite of your toppling ice cream sundae, so I'll repeat that. GOD BELIEVES IN YOU!

I like how Bob Goff puts it, in reference to God's view of us, "He doesn't grimace at our failures, He delights in our attempts."

So, adversity is a punk and is on the prowl to destroy our moments and, eventually, our lives. But remember that God has put limits on it, not the other way around, so let us live with that powerful expectancy. Let us thrive and push forward with the most secure hope we can possess. Embrace God's love and let Him hold you through your storm.

HOPE...*Rises*

Like a powerful sunrise that breaks through the cluttered scene, hope rises again and again.
Something as majestic as a sunrise continues to bring a sense of awe at the beginning of our day. The glimpse of its appearance begins early when the darkest part of the night fades away against the brilliance of light that approaches. Nocturnal skies succumb to the day and begin to conceal its brilliant stars behind a heavy cloak, to slumber throughout the coming hours of perfect sunlight. Until I witnessed the magnificent Milky Way galaxy from near the top of Mauna Kea in Hawaii, I had no understanding of the vast reach and explosive sparkle of our heavenly stars.
And yet, the incredible array of brilliance is gently swept away by the sunlight's scenic broom as if to make ready for the coming of its power. Then, like the many times before with perfect consistency, the sun's might

crests over the still horizon and rises to greet us. That's what Hope does.

HOPE...Has No Expiration Date

There's no time limit with true hope—it doesn't expire. It outlasts the worst of situations and outlives the enemy of misery. It has life and breath, but never dies; it's ongoing and has a persistent heartbeat that never quits.

Unlike the time constraints of each and every twenty-four hour period, hope doesn't rise and fall in the course of a flight. Nor does it require a climb or a descent; it has no end or cycle. Even our most wonderful days come to an end and they may even string together a course of memories that lighten our hearts, but the hope that breathes life into a weary soul has no end.

Psalm 71:5 says, "O Lord, you alone are my hope. I've trusted you, O Lord, from childhood." And I can say these very words because they hold true for me.

Eight years old was a fantastic time for me. I had the blessing of being rescued by God when I became of follower of Jesus Christ. Even though I had no life experience like most young adults, mid-life adults or those more advanced in age, I still realized that I needed Him.

At this point in my childhood, I was a boy raised in a divorced family, broken. Yet, I was blessed with loving parents even though their marital status had ended.

As a young child, I sometimes thought about why my parents were no longer together. I mean they were still Mom and Dad to me, but not in the same household. As an only child, there was just so much available time to ponder these types of things and weigh them in my heart. I didn't want to consider the cause for their separation, but I couldn't help to think that perhaps I was a reason for that separation. Although looking back now, I know that idea was just a lie from the enemy of my soul.

So, here comes God in His most delightful superhero manner to scoop me up and rescue me. He rushed in to save my days and I knew exactly what I was doing when I asked Him to take my life. Whether at age eight or eighty, God has the ability to transform lives and drape His perfect peace over our existence.

As years became periods of time, as we see mile markers on an endless highway, I faced heartaches that we all meet during adolescent years. When these heartaches ambushed my peace, my hope persisted...my hope in God that I received when I was rescued in 1976 as an 8-year-old.

Periodically, when other valleys of darkness surrounded my life, I remembered that hope was still there for me. It was present and alive; it was powerful and had never died. Year after year the story of timeless hope continued. Because when hope has no expiration date, that is exactly what it means—it cannot and will not ever expire. Like an Everlasting Gobstopper (thank you, Mr. Willy Wonka, for that great metaphor), that juicy flavor of powerful and unending hope lasts and lasts and lasts.

HOPE...*Reaches*

I look up and find a break in the heavy clouds. Through the ominous curtains that fold within themselves with vapors of silvery crème, I see a stretch of deep blue and it reminds me of the hope I hold onto. And when I see with hopeful eyes, my heart reaches for You.
During those days when grief, pain, and sorrow try to overtake me, I remember You are my strength and my song. I take refuge in the shadow of Your wing. When my feet are heavy and I feel paralyzed, it is Your love that reaches for me.

Roger R. Ziegler

HOPE...*Soars*

Hope soars on high. It carries and it lifts me up. - Isaiah 40:31

I remember as a youngster one of my simple pleasures was kite flying. This basic exercise in wind physics and gravity meant I would be able to enjoy staring up into the wide-open sky to my plastic colorful glider for upwards of over an hour. No electronics present. No power supply required. But it was pure fun.

The best part of the whole experience was probably selecting my favorite design. Because they ranged anywhere from soaring eagles with spread open wings and its talons at the ready, to a superhero, like Superman in his favorite pose on the underside. When the kite soared into the atmosphere whatever animal, character or colorful pattern I chose would hang over my part of the city where I lived, so very high up in the air. It was sort of like my proud banner waving and hovering in the wind for all to see.

The Hope Parade

There were times when the spool of the string provided with the kite was simply not enough. Why? Because all of its fifty feet was used up and there were no additional reserves left for newer heights. So, I would always have at least one pal with me and either that person or someone they could summons for help would provide some of their own string. Another spool was brought with haste by a dispatched sprinter and I began to graft the new spool of string into the existing one attached to the kite. It was accomplished by a super special knot, sort of like NASA uses in their space program, and I would unravel the next spool of string slowly. It was terrific when the plan worked.

Now my kite was able to extend further and further away from earth. I was concerned that a strong gust of wind would create enough force and bust the string through the plastic fastener at the kite's underside. But after a while, it soared so high into the deep blue skies that it was hardly visible. It looked like a mere speck to our eyes.

Then we got really creative. We grabbed a used small paper bag, usually from a nearby store or McDonald's (because we most often found ourselves standing in the rear parking lot of this fast-food restaurant) and created a wind sail. A clean tear was made along the length of the paper bag and into the base so that it ended directly in the center of the bottom of the bag. Then we used some magic clear tape (same stuff NASA uses, I'm sure) and performed our task.

The bag was carefully placed onto the tight string through the tear until it reached the end of the opening. Then we taped the tear so that it regained its original bag shape. When we were done, the bag was positioned open end facing me sort of like a parachute and it was evenly secured with the string right through its center. Perfect! We looked at each other as if this was some momentous occasion, then we released the paper bag. The wind began to carry our homemade sail upwards several inches at a time until it was being carried away towards the kite hundreds of feet skyward. *"Whoa!"* we would exhale.

It was an amazing sight for sure. With every stronger gust of wind, the bag carried higher and soared greater. And that's how hope is. When the circumstances are huge, hope just soars higher over it and carries our hearts to a place that is amazing. It doesn't even rely on our own supply of string or a nearby friend for theirs.

Roger R. Ziegler

When you find yourself facing the walls of despair, hope will lift and help you to soar.

HOPE... *Illuminates*

In the shadow of fear, hope illuminates. Because fear can bring looming clouds filled with doom and oppressive gloom, it can be overwhelming and distressful. The climate of our surroundings becomes dull and spackled with coarse gray hedges.
Suddenly, a brilliant radiance appears and it's meant for our deliverance. It causes the darkness and the cold fear to scatter; the gloomy landscape evaporates at the immediate illumination. What once was a moment beneath a heavy shadow, now becomes a radiant episode like no other.
Hope is a brilliant radiance.
The Lord is my light... Psalm 27:1.

Roger R. Ziegler

Bully

In 1987 I received a shocking phone call from my childhood best friend. Jesse Saenz was my pal who stood by my side through elementary and junior high school years. We both lived in East Los Angeles and in the same neighborhood—the city called Huntington Park. On this day, his unexpected phone call shook my life.

Our apartment buildings were separated by a house covered with massive trees and thousands of various sized leaves. They provided a tremendous amount of shade for this house's back yard, where a couple of angry little dogs had roamed, and the foliage also blocked my direct view of Jesse's apartment from my bedroom window. Otherwise, I'm certain that we would have communicated through flashlight signals or other visible methods.

As kids, we explored the wonders of city life in a congested urban setting. We both were a part of a larger group of pals we ran with,

The Hope Parade

but he was my best friend from the group. At the end of the day, Jesse was the one who I would later keep in touch with after moving out of that neighborhood years later. We swapped Vans sneakers (when they first became a popular line of casual footwear) and shocked our junior high peers with our captivating style. We both definitely rocked our 1980-82 years by unique designs this line of footwear had offered.

One time we swapped one shoe for the day, Vans of course. I wore his left and he wore my left. My pair at the time were dark blue, canvas "tie-ups" with white laces and his were stark white, canvas "slip-on" style. We each wore one white and one blue shoe the entire school day. We were bold like that and bucked the trends!

One day as sixth graders we walked to school together and each held our bibles proudly along the sidewalk. He had recently given his life to Jesus. Jesse heard about my Lord through the same bible stories I was told and he realized a savior was what he needed—even as a sixth-grader He heard the same music that I had listened to and liked it. Songs from Keith Green, Leon Patillo, and The Resurrection Band were some of my favorites. Jesse related to the lyrics and they had a special meaning to him.

I think Jesse was a softie on the inside. He revealed a sensitive and caring heart when we were not around the group of guys. After all, the Jesse that mostly everyone else knew was a fighter who wouldn't stand down from anyone no matter the size of the opponent. And because he was into boxing, he could deliver punishment with his fists at will. He usually reserved that side of him for bullies. He didn't like them.

In the middle of my freshman year of high school, our family moved out of the unruly streets of East Los Angeles to an inland suburb on the outskirts of L.A. County. I left behind the streets I roamed for over ten years as a youngster and also moved away from my pals I grew up with, including Jesse. We kept in touch with phone calls and visits on some weekends. But at some point later in our high school years, we lost touch. Those things happen. We would always be close pals, no matter the distance circumstance.

Shortly after my high school graduation in 1986, I moved two hours south to live with my father in San Diego. Living with divorced parents had its disadvantages and some holes to fill, so I jumped at the opportunity to live with him and sort of catch up—make up for the lost time that every other weekend could not satisfy in my younger years.

It was during 1987 while in San Diego when I received a call that disturbed me. It was from Jesse, my pal from those early days exploring East LA adventures. After a few words, he got right to the point of his call. He began to tell me how he was afflicted with aggressive cancer in his stomach area. A tumor had grown to the size of a softball was how he described it to me and he needed intense treatment that included surgery. My heart sank deeply. My mind raced back to memories of seeing his smile and how he would have no problem facing a bully or two. This was no different. Only this time the bully was not some punk who picked on a weaker person or who called someone nasty names to hurt them. No, this time it was end-stage cancer that served a full course meal of misery to my best friend's life. I hate it when that happens.

It didn't take more than a day for me to jump in my truck and drive north on the I-5 Freeway for a couple of hours. I couldn't get to the hospital soon enough and reunite with Jesse. When I reached the busy L.A. traffic I knew I was not far away. Finally, I pulled into the hospital's parking structure and found a spot. As I walked impatiently through the brightly lit halls I felt a nervousness invade my heart. Suddenly, my emotions became stale and a lifeless gaze fell over my face as if I inadvertently pulled a mask down to conceal my real identity. The elevator ride to his floor was so quiet I could hear paint dry. Oddly, I sensed the reality of what was about to occur—my best friend was about to be seen in his worst physical state of health and I didn't know if I was ready for that.

I stepped out of the elevator and into the oncology floor. With the help of a nurse, I was directed to my friend's quarters. Without hesitation, I walked up to the doorway of his room and peeked inside. Jesse's eyes met mine from his hospital bed where he rested and he flashed a big smile. I walked over and greeted him with our homeboy, "East L.A. handshake" and my warmest hug. My friend looked tired, weathered and very sick. He was just a shadow of the person I remembered before.

The Hope Parade

As he told me about his recent medical battles, I kept my attention directly on his eyes. My peripheral vision picked up on obvious clues that screamed how sick he was. His bald head and missing eyebrows were evidence of chemotherapy in addition to his sunken-in eye sockets. His olive-brown skin tone now looked pasty and pale. I remembered him standing tall with his six-foot frame, but that was now deceptive because his weight loss made his shoulders appear frail. He was weak and extremely tired. The bully revealed as cancer was persistent and kept pounding Jesse with blow after blow.

I was crushed, but I kept my pain to myself. Instead, I grinned and listened with heartfelt intention to understand every detail. I missed my pal so much, but it wasn't until I sat there by his bedside that I completely realized the enormity. We shared stories and we both asked how each other's families were doing. And there was no place I would rather have been than right by his side. It was the perfect place to be.

After a long conversation and a few laughs, I asked him if he was ready to go home. We both knew that I didn't mean his address back in Huntington Park, right there on Marbrisa Street. Rather, we both understood that I meant Heaven—his new address to come. He smiled really big, like a towering large order of french fries from Spartan Burger—our childhood hangout. Then he said with perfect peace, "Yeah. I met with the hospital chaplain and made sure I am ready to see Jesus." The weight of those calm words he spoke could be felt like a warm blanket on a snowy night. Because here was my best friend in the whole world who I was blessed to grow up with and he was about to embark on a journey not seen with human eyes. A journey towards his permanent residence to a place where there will be no more pain and Jesus will wipe away every tear. That comforts me and it sure comforted my pal.

After a beautiful visit, I began my drive back to San Diego. Jesse filled my every thought like I was watching movies of our times together. I regretted not seeing him more frequently over the previous couple of years. I should have made the drive and made the effort. The ride home was long and I was filled with melancholy and sadness. It shook me. I didn't want to see my friend in the condition he was in and it became the last time I looked into his eyes.

Jesse passed on not long after our visit. Almost as if my being there was the last thing he wanted to check off on a list of things to do before taking his last breath. At least I'd like to think so. I think he cared for me just as much as I did for him and our last time together sort of gave each other permission to move forward. For him, he was about to enter eternity. For me, I was about to continue my journey on this planet and continue to do this thing called "Life." And I was ready to take his memory with me along for the long ride.

The funeral service was nicely done and honored my best friend very well. I was able to see his kind mother and his siblings. Warm embraces and tears were the best things we shared with each other. It was a difficult day for everyone and I can only imagine the jabs of pain Jesse's mother had felt along with waves of overwhelming grief. I hoped that I never had to experience such a loss in my life. I don't think I could ever handle such a terrible hole in my existence.

Jesse became a loving memory I often recall. Sharing a burger and fries as our favorite songs played on the jukebox while at Spartan Burger, playing football on our street lined with parked cars in our congested neighborhood, and laughing hysterically at the humor we both found in many commonalities were just some of the samples I dipped my mind into. It was a tough loss as an eighteen-year-old to burden and I never forgot that peaceful look on his face when he told me he was ready to go home. It was pure hope.

Because even during the most daunting and difficult situation that bullied him, he experienced the powerful joy of *The Hope Parade*. And it marched right through the middle of that Los Angeles hospital, with a rumble of uplifting cheer and quite possibly a fresh pair of different colored Vans for my best friend to wear in Heaven. One white shoe and one blue shoe, of course.

HOPE...*Persists*

Hope—it persists. And it continues firmly through every strenuous affliction, opposition, or barrage. When the seemingly unending and silent, cold fear stalks, remember the hope that defends also shadows you in comfort. No matter the course—steady or unstable—hope outlasts in spite of difficulty.

Although the present darkness may convince you of defeat, it is the soon coming daylight that anchors our hearts in what is true and sure. Just as the daylight always returns to announce a brand new day, so does hope reside within the context of persistence.

Roger R. Ziegler

Man In the Clouds

The thief on the cross experienced hope at the final hour of his life. Think about it. He hung there as a criminal of society who deserved death and he was ready to breathe his last knowing full well of his fate. He received his punishment publicly. He had no chance to be taken down off of this cross of torture and somehow be pardoned. He was defeated by the criminal justice system, rightly so, and he only had time left to reflect upon the decisions that put him there.

Suddenly, he was in the presence of the most powerful person in history. Wonderfully, he was only one of two people who were right beside the savior of humanity. Little did he know that his eternal future was about to change because of who hung on a cross just several feet away from his very own. Because Jesus became a ransom for us and was the Lamb of God who took away the sin of the world.

The Hope Parade

Including the ones belonging to the thieves on the cross to His left and to His right.

As one thief was perched high above the crowds who anxiously gathered to witness firsthand the Roman execution, he realized something extraordinary. Now he was eye-level with the King of Kings and the Lord of Lords. His heart raced with the fear of his looming entrance to eternal doom. Without words, he gazed upon a loving Savior. Tears began to blur his waning vision as his own reality and his feeble kingdom came crashing down. His humanity was no match for the judgment to come. The release of sweet surrender imposed its will on a sinful pride that fell victim to God's perfect love.

You see, the thief was a man, a human, the same as we are. And beneath the rough exterior lived a soul who cried out for mercy. A soul that craved peace, but was shackled in irons of destruction permanently. A soul destined for judgment and punishment for not embracing salvation from God himself. A soul created to have a beautiful relationship with our Creator. And just like all of us, he required forgiveness. Not from society, but from Jesus himself.

With his outstretched hands, Jesus hung there bleeding, violently beaten, and wickedly bruised for our iniquities; despised by the world and forsaken by all. Delivered by his own hand with willful submission to the Father and into the hands of his persecutors. Innocent, but our transgressions he bore upon himself. Perfect in his humanity, he paid dearly for the price of our sins. He paid with his life. And for the criminal's life as well.

Perhaps he heard about Jesus during the last few years of His ministry. Maybe he knew about the miraculous works and powerful gestures of grace. Or saw Him with multitudes gathering by the Sea of Galilea and possibly he was one of those who ate from the supernatural fish and loaves blessing. Maybe he witnessed Jesus overturn tables at the temple as the house of God was defiled. Maybe he witnessed from just a few feet away from the triumphant entry into Jerusalem as Jesus rode on the back of a donkey—just maybe.

Yeah, that's very possible. But the point here is that it's not enough to just believe in Him or be a witness of His miracles or agree with the masses that Jesus Christ is an important figure in history.

No, you can't just be a fan or a verbal supporter. The thief himself realized this and took his life one important step further which made all of the difference in his own eternity.

Because on the surface, there was a criminal charged and convicted by the courts, yet beneath his exterior, there was another conflict. That being his own struggle with humanity and his sinful state. You could say that he was in fear for his future—no, not a physical one because that fate was sealed at the hand of the fierce Roman persecutors. They didn't make mistakes in their torture regimen—ever. The fact that he hung there on a cross next to Jesus says it all.

He had very little time left to breathe due to extreme torture. He painfully gasped to feed his lungs that were strained because of the mere positioning of his body. Exhaustion and dehydration were evident on his face and demeanor. Suffering was certain and visible. On the surface, the thief only had moments left to decide.

As the crowds beneath them watched these three men die before their very eyes, the thief knew in his heart he deserved this form of punishment—death on a cross. His thoughts raced as time continued to expire. His breathing increasingly became shallow and rapid. He stared down at those who he at one time engaged within social circles with and a people who now, because of his own crimes, distanced themselves from him in his final hours.

He felt as though the distance that separated him from these people, the world below, was more than only feet or yards. Instead, it felt as though his separation was a vast span in his moment of condemnation; a chasm or a massive interval between him and humanity. He felt aggressively pushed away like a rotten pile of disgust. Like a man evicted into the atmosphere—fiercely outcast into the clouds.

And just like a swift change in the course of the desert winds across the land, in merely a moment, he made a decision. When his circumstance was barren with any glimpse of life or peace, hope itself broke through his despair. He turned to Jesus who hung directly across from him, also perched high above the earth and was tortured beyond recognition. He yielded to a calling of the Holy Spirit to embrace the forgiveness offered by God in the flesh for all mankind...

including the likeness of a thief. He believed from the deepest parts of his human heart and with every fiber of his being that Jesus was the Son of God.

In a public defense, he looked across from Jesus to the other criminal facing the same physical destruction and told him Christ was completely innocent, unlike themselves. His reverence for God was apparent in his words as well. Then, he focused on Jesus and spoke those amazing words of belief:

"Jesus, remember me when you come into your Kingdom." And with grace and mercy from the One who died for all of mankind, Jesus replied:

"I assure you, today you will be with me in paradise."

It was perfect hope delivered from a perfect God-Man named Jesus Christ. If we were there, I'm certain that the forgiven thief wore a countenance of peace that only God can impute and we would be able to visibly see its evidence. Because he knew for the first time in his adult life that his eternal future was solidified, secured, and delivered by the very One who he would spend eternity with.

Hope didn't arrive too late. Hope didn't hide from the darkness of his worst circumstances. Hope destroyed the very fear this man was shackled to and brought a Parade of Joy, Peace, and Assurance... and it was free for the taking.

The man in the clouds was separated from society, punished by a crucifixion death, and he was outcast because of his crimes but was also released into Heaven upon his death. It was the very hope of Jesus that ushered him into Paradise. A place far beyond the clouds.

HOPE...*Pierces fear*

HOPE. It pierces and permeates the dark cloud of fear. It reaches down during the most intense adversity and not only takes our hand but embraces our life. It's powerful, unending and for everyone.

Yet during those sinister attacks delivered by our enemy of fear, we have the ability to escape the snare diabolically set for us. The calm of perfect peace, the tranquil comfort knowing our lives are secure in our Master's hand, and the brilliance of His joy overshadows the feeble attempts fear makes to distract us. Even though we possess the ability, we must not lay down our defense and our strategies to stand firm.

And when we are surrounded by these disturbing clouds, fear's appearance within a beautiful moment, it is always the enormous, brilliant power of hope that pierces despair and shines directly through to our hearts. We become embraced by the assurance that removes any doubts left behind. Because when the deepest, darkest night falls, we have the light of Christ to illuminate every aspect of our precious lives.

Roger R. Ziegler

Dante

It was a rainy, winter Sunday morning in 1992. I kissed Paula and baby Shelby goodbye as I left our apartment, headed for church. Because Shelby was still an infant, we kept her home until she was a little older. We both suffered from the new and young parent syndrome (I was 23 and Paula was 22). We were convinced she would contract some exotic disease for sure.

I hurried to my truck, a 1984 rust-orange Nissan, to avoid getting doused by the rain. But it was a failed attempt. I climbed in, started the engine and wiped my face with my wet hands. I think we owned an umbrella but that was at home. I pulled out of our apartment complex and headed down Valley View to pick up my sister-in-law, Lisa. We often carpooled to church, but on this day it would exclude Paula.

I had maybe a fifteen-minute drive to her place then we had a long drive to Calvary Chapel West Covina—a nice 30-minute

The Hope Parade

commute at minimum. But what I didn't know that morning was that an alternate plan was already scheduled for me. God does that in His unique way.

After several minutes into my drive, I was startled by a very loud noise that sounded like a shotgun blast that came from the engine compartment. Boom! The truck immediately lost power and the engine died. I steered the vehicle to the right and stopped against the curb on Valley View in La Mirada. The rain continued to fall and there were really very few cars on the road.

It was 1992, so I didn't have the luxury of pulling out my cell phone to call for help. I jumped out of the driver's side and popped open the hood. And there it was—a car battery murdered by some scientific paradox. It looked as if a Xenomorph exploded out from the belly of this old battery. But this was reality and I was not the main character in some Ridley Scott motion picture. After my quick and obvious assessment, I jumped back in the cab and closed the door.

Stranded. In the rain. Now what? Do I walk to the nearest payphone to make a call for assistance? I sat there thinking how bad this situation was because this was our only vehicle and we didn't possess one of those money trees I hear about in many fables; we didn't have much in terms of resources. I asked God for His help and I sat there paused in my day, held captive by circumstance. The rainfall was steady and continuous. It made visibility tough to see through the dense layers of moisture beyond my windshield. But not enough to see an oncoming car suddenly appear from behind, several car lengths back.

At first, I thought maybe it was a patrol car; a police officer stopping to check on my abandoned situation or my odd choice of parking along such a large road. Then I turned my head around to get a better look through my rear cab window and realized it was not a first responder at all. No, it was a white car slowly pulling to the curb behind my truck. The vehicle came to a stop directly behind me alongside the curb. I couldn't make out the occupants because of the steady rain, so I sat there motionless. Almost immediately, I saw someone exit their driver's side and briskly walk over to my side of the truck. I cranked my window down with the lever (there were no power windows or other fancy accessories in my Nissan). A young guy, around my age, approached my door and asked me if I was alright.

"Hi, Yeah, I'm stranded. My battery just exploded," I said. "There was a loud boom sound from the engine and it just died." He looked puzzled.

He walked to the front of the truck and lifted the hood. I joined him to see if he had any ideas because I was not so sure of myself when it came to cars.

"Wow," he was shocked to see the blown-up battery. "You're gonna need a new one, but everything else looks okay." He was calming and confident.

"I just don't have any money for this and I was about to call someone to help," I explained.

Without hesitation he offered assistance. "I'll help you. Get in my car and I'll drive you."

"Really? I would really appreciate that," I said. I was moved by his generosity, especially because I was a stranger. Besides, who stops in the middle of a storm to check on a stranded driver? I guess there are quite a few good citizens, but he made the effort and I was about to get blessed more than what I had expected.

He gently dropped the hood of my Nissan and he told me to climb in his car. I rolled up my window and jogged back to his waiting car. It was a 4-door, older model than my truck and had black wheels that perhaps once adorned hubcaps. I sat in the passenger side and saw a young child standing on the back seat. His smile was contagious. The seats were worn pretty well and the basic model Nissan I drove suddenly felt like a high end, luxurious truck by comparison. This car was barely hanging on.

Moments later the guy climbed back into his car behind the steering wheel. Across the stiff bench seat to my left sat a soaking wet stranger who had the largest smile plastered on his face. He officially introduced himself.

"Hey, I'm Dante and this is my son," he said with an upbeat tone.

"I'm Roger. Nice to meet you," I answered. "I really do appreciate your help with this." I glanced back and smiled at his 4-year-old son.

The Hope Parade

Dante had very short hair that made him look like he was bald and he had a stocky, muscular build on his 5'-6" frame. He wiped his head with a large towel that was kept on the seat next to him, then he began to wipe down the inside of the fogged up windshield. He didn't have a good working defroster system, so he was forced to wipe the glass on his own...every few minutes. Although, It didn't seem to bother him. His happy demeanor was too much for circumstances to handle.

The car sputtered as we drove away from the curb. The wiper blades were engaged but didn't help the view through the windshield very much. It was one of those kinds of storms. I asked him where we were headed and he told me back to his place. He explained further that he needed to pick up something from his apartment.

We had a nice conversation during the ten-minute journey. He shared his dream to become a Deputy Sheriff and how he was in the testing process. I told him that was something I thought about pursuing as well. But most of all, his words were seasoned with Jesus and his love for the Lord. As we pulled up to his apartment, I felt like I was bathed in grace and mercy just by his speech.

He asked me to join him and his son; he wanted me to meet his wife who was home. After our introductions, he slipped away into a rear part of the home for a few minutes. His wife was just as sweet as he was. In fact this entire family and household were uplifting. For that short time at Dante's place, I forgot I had a broken-down truck and I was right in the middle of adversity. It's funny how that happens.

"You ready to roll, Roger?" Dante asked as he came back into the living room.

"Yeah. Let's go," I answered then turned to his wife and thanked her for hospitality. Her smile sent us off, back into the rainy day.

I sat in his car and noticed he had trouble with a stuck door handle and tugged on the door to get it open. It was in such bad condition and was the only vehicle his family had. Interestingly, Dante didn't say one negative thing about it. He just continued to smile, wipe the inside of the foggy windshield and told me how wonderful Jesus was.

"Where to now?" I asked.

"We're going to the auto parts store for your battery," he quickly replied. As if there was nowhere else we needed to be going.

"Thanks, but I don't have any money."

"Don't worry about that," his words were reassuring. "I have enough to help."

I was grateful for his kindness. "Thank you, Dante."

Then it hit me. He probably went home to grab some money for the part I needed. I sensed a hope that unexpectedly invaded my day and it was smothered in grins and declarations of how wonderful Jesus was. Even his sidekick, his little boy perched atop the back seat, still wore the biggest smile. I'm telling you, that family was something else.

As we drove through the drenched streets, Dante explained how right before he saw my truck along the road he was headed to church. He was compelled by God to offer his help. I love that he was available for such a business...Kingdom business. He handled his life in such a way that no matter the odd details of such inconvenience, he was ready to be God's hands and feet.

We drove up to the auto parts store, picked out a shiny new battery and then he pulled out cash from his pocket to pay for it at the counter. Our final stretch brought us back to my helpless Nissan. And of course, Dante gave me the red carpet treatment by reinstalling it under the hood.

"Go ahead and start it up," he said. "You should be good now."

And with a turn of my key and every bit of power delivered by that terrific battery, the engine started. It was instantly brought back to life.

"Man, I really appreciate all of your help today," I said to my new friend as I shook his hand.

"I'm glad I was able to help, Roger. God took care of you today," he said. "God bless you."

And within a couple of minutes, Dante drove off into the canopy of falling rain. Our adventure must have occupied at least an hour of the morning and most definitely sidetracked me from going to church. But I felt like the most blessed man on the planet. I was supercharged and energized by that encounter. "Thank you, Jesus!" I shouted as I headed home, back to Paula and Shelby.

The Hope Parade

When I got back to our apartment, I explained how my morning went and she was amazed. We called Lisa to let her know what had occurred because I'm sure she was waiting for a while. She too was praising the Lord for His goodness.

I was grateful for Dante. I was especially thankful for God's provision. That day sat with me for a long while, right in my heart. It was a moving expression of love. But little did I know it would not be the last time I would see Dante or be touched by God's powerful hope.

~

It was an exciting time. The month of August 1993, was filled with beautiful expectancy. It was the end of Paula's second pregnancy and she was about to deliver our second child. It was the 19th and a very special day.

I parked our truck in the emergency room lot and grabbed a wheelchair for her. We checked in to the main desk at Western Medical Center located in Santa Ana, CA and a nurse brought her to the labor and delivery room. I ran back to the truck and moved it to the guest parking structure. I was feeling pretty excited right about then and I waited for the elevator impatiently to reach the floor. The doors parted and I turned towards the "baby launch" zone.

All of a sudden, he was there. It was Dante, my car battery savior. Our eyes met and we shook hands.

"Hey, Roger! What are you doing here?" he asked. He wore green scrubs and a name tag. He had that same massive smile just like the year before.

"Hi, Dante! We're having a baby and my wife's in the labor room."

"Wow. Congratulations! As you can see, I work here right now, but I'm still trying to get into the Sheriffs."

I was happy to see him but more thrilled to get back to Paula. We said goodbye and I hurried to my bride. It was a big lift for my heart, seeing Dante just before the birth of our second child. I was reminded of the rainy day in early 1992 when hope found me helpless on Valley View Blvd. The act of love and grace from a stranger was what I needed that desperate day. But, I didn't know that hours after arriving at the hospital our lives would be rocked by something unexpected in that delivery room. It was no accident that I was met by Dante in that hallway.

After a long and rough labor, Paula gave birth to our son, Noah. Within seconds of his arrival, chaos ensued and adversity called our number. You see, Noah was born with a condition called Gastroschisis. His small and large intestines were outside of his body and his belly was closed; the rest of his organs were safely tucked away inside just like they were supposed to be. Yet, his entire intestinal tract was somehow ignored. As if his body rejected it and turned its back on it in the womb.

I was in a state of horror and nearly frozen. Paula kept asking what was wrong because the team rushed our son across the room to tend to him, urgently. Baby Noah was immediately taken to a waiting ambulance where he was driven a few miles to Children's Hospital of Orange County for emergency surgery. His life was on the line and our hearts felt like they were sentenced to death.

As I kissed Paula ever so gently and told her everything was going to be alright, I had to leave her there to be by Noah's side. I began a short and painful drive to Children's Hospital. The few miles were not what I had expected them to be. No, the drive felt like decades and pure torture as my "daddy's heart" was pounding to escape my chest cavity. I experienced tunnel vision wondering what would happen to our little Noah.

But, God showed Himself even before Paula's intense labor began. By bringing Dante to me, out of all the places and all of the times, he showed up on our worst day ever. In essence, Dante equaled hope. He represented the glorious expectation found within our darkest moments. Yes, he was an ambassador of the most powerful and perfect hope that exists. The hope provided by Jesus.

I waited there in that empty hospital room, desperate and afraid. During those stressful, pre-dawn hours, I held onto the only fabric of hope I had. The surgery lasted centuries, so it seemed and I could only think of how Paula must have felt held captive in her separate hospital room, recovering from giving birth. I wish I could be in both places at once.

The Hope Parade

Finally, news from the surgeon filled me with gratitude. Our little baby was out of danger. The procedure was successful and he was now ready to mend, to find rest in recovery. The physician explained how they were able to place all of Noah's small and large intestines carefully back into his body cavity, which is rare for this type of situation. He was sutured and patched up with great skill. My exhale was felt throughout the floor, I'm certain of it.

Over the next four weeks, Paula and I remained at his side as he was a patient of the Neo-natal Intensive Care Unit. A patient. Now that term should only be kept locked away for adults who find themselves more advanced in age, not newborn children put in a deadly chokehold by this world at day one. And looking back on those days, it was his induction to a life smattered with medical adversity the likes very few would ever see. We held him and we loved every part of his young life. Our hearts melted with his and formed a bond that could never be broken.

Dante was placed within two separate important days in my journey of life. You see, it was powerful hope—like a parade—that in its most wonderful fanfare, uplifting sense, and joyful abundance came to me. No matter the outcome of my circumstances I knew that my life was held in God's hand and everything would be fashioned by His purpose. And that is an exceptional place to live.

Our environment and life's most difficult moments cannot separate us from the love of God. Never. I often need to be reminded when my surroundings bully my peace. Whether a busted-up car battery or my son introduced to life by diabolical illness, God's love soothes an aching heart. And sometimes he uses a stranger with a massive smile to do so; sometimes his name is Dante.

His word doesn't tell us we would be free from despair or withheld from times of misery—both big and small. No, it's not the message God intended to deliver to us, His beloved. Let's not kid ourselves into thinking life's filled with pancakes and extra blueberry syrup every single day. We often will be served the meals that are actually good for us. You know, the ones made with extra helpings of nutrient-dense vegetables and other vitamin-rich foods we sometimes ignore. Not always tasty to our sweet-tooth, brainwashed taste buds. And when those trials come upon us let us remember they present opportunities for our growth, as James points out in scripture—James 1:2-4. We always want a mountain of extra sweet pancakes and never the kale and spinach salad we probably should eat instead.

HOPE... *Is contagious*

The many are affected by the one. Why not make that experience wonderful?
When authentic love is displayed that carves through our culture with ease and delivers a firm trust, the results are infectious. At a minimum, we can easily be confused by the clutter of the world's ideas outside of God's word. So it becomes vital to bathe our minds, our hearts in His life-changing scripture. We will be transformed by a renewing of our mind and a rich development within our character will manifest.
It is by His enrichment within our lives, we will become fruit-bearers in a world lacking in nutrient-dense spiritual food. Hearts longing for rescue will become attracted to the hope flowing through us. And our newness of joy and the love that dwells within us will infect those around us. Our outward display of hope will always be contagious.

HOPE...*Ignites*

Sometimes we need a spark to set life ablaze within our hearts. To burn away the cobwebs and eliminate the turmoil of past years; to eradicate emotional baggage that anchors us down; to release our hearts from that which prevents our flight.
The warmth of the campfire glow needs a beginning. The downtown street marquee discovers its luminescence with a turn of a switch. And sometimes we require a flash, a burst of ignition within us to crank our motion and stoke the inferno of our next victory. Let the God of Heaven be the hope that sparks and ignites you. Flames, like vibrant colors, will arise.

In Sickness and In Health

The news caught me by surprise. I'm sure the same has happened to you at some point as well. It was 2014 during the latter part of October when my bride, Princess Paula, went to a medical appointment. She was fighting some illness symptoms as a result of mold exposure in our previous home's basement. We moved into a different house once the shocking discovery was realized. The visit was intended to examine and assess, but the unthinkable exposed itself instead.

It was cancer. Yeah, the "C" word, the bully of our era. And it now became as real as the air she breathed on a daily basis. They discovered a mass in her left breast and, after nearly a four-hour visit with all of the necessary tests, the doctor informed her that it had been present for about four to five years. It was a slow-growth type with an appetite specifically for estrogen.

I was at the office when she sent me a text message. I expected different and less alarming information. The words across my screen caused me to stand and walk to an empty room immediately. My finger dialed her cell number as I hurried to a quiet area. I was lightheaded.

Paula's voice was calm but carried an eerie tone that was consistent with our dialogue surrounding our son's ongoing and life-threatening condition. "The doctor found cancer in my left breast." Those words stunned me instantly and I stood paralyzed both literally in the physical and emotional sense, down to the very center of my core. *No! No!* I thought to myself. *Not this. Not Paula. Not now.*

After a solemn conversation, we ended the call and agreed to meet back at our home. I could hear the evidence of pure silence ringing in both ears. A vast nothingness suffocated my upbeat tempo and chased away my usual grin. I asked myself if this was a dream, like many times and for so many years before with our son, Noah. Reality answered back because it read my mind and overheard my unspoken question. This was as real as it gets.

I walked with haste back to my desk and grabbed my keys. The first real conversation I had was with my boss, our V.P. of Sales, inside of his office. I choked the words out of my mouth and I was sure they were somewhat clear and conveyed my message. My intention was to leave abruptly and get home as soon as I possibly could. He understood and expressed his shock and concern.

It was about 3:30 that day with very little traffic flow in my general direction. I felt like the 25-minute drive was accompanied by an autopilot feature, because my mind kept flooding with volumes of related memories, thoughts, and moments rather than focusing on the task of driving a vehicle. My stomach felt as though a cage fighter had punched me square in my abdomen and I could barely swallow because of raw emotion that welled up from inside.

I just couldn't believe this was happening to us. It seemed like blow after blow continued to pound our family, like waves upon waves fuming with anger. And to see my wife's beautiful face in my head as I drove to our home was difficult, knowing that soon I would be holding her and sharing an embrace steeped with pain. We always had each other to lean on during our marriage and we kept wonderful lines of communication open.

When I stepped through the door, the house was empty—I arrived first. A few minutes later she pulled up and parked in front. Once she was inside the living room, we held each other for a long while. We shed tears of hurt, of sorrow, of shock, and of uncertainty. I told her how sorry I was and that I would be with her every moment through the fight ahead.

The plan to remove the cancer was incorporated with action to move swiftly because the disease had encamped within her body for a number of years. They officially gave her a Stage 3C diagnosis, which meant the cells had spread to other portions of her body. This included her lymphatic system, an expressway to her entire body, and other nearby tissues.

Thanksgiving 2014 was one of those holidays where our family gathered around a lovely meal and expressed our thankfulness to our Lord for His blessings. After all, we had extreme amounts of blessings to appreciate considering the enormity of what we had experienced with our son's medical situation since he was born in 1993. Our outlook was shaped by a lens crafted by Jesus and His beautiful love for each and every one of us specifically. And there are no boundaries to His magnificent love.

Paula just had her port installed. It was smartly placed beneath her skin, located in her upper chest near her collar bone. It was going to be used for her chemotherapy infusions for the next several months. Thanksgiving dinner—Thursday evening—was a special time for her and for us. Because her first treatment would be administered that coming Monday. But that night would be spent with her children and with loved ones who came across the country to support our family.

We knew it was the calm before the storm that so many of us hear about. Either in the movies, on TV, or in our discussions with others, we understood what this expression meant. The calm had settled on our lives just as we prepared for the calamity my wife would endure very soon. There was peace and there was hope. Not the kind you buy at the local thrift store from a dusty shelf for a buck fifty. No, the kind of hope that is stored in Heaven for such a time as this. And we knew the punch line. It was this: no matter the outcome, Paula would be personally cared for and escorted through the fire by our loving and gracious God. How can anything stand against that? Nothing. Period.

~

As expected, the chemotherapy infusions delivered chaos and misery to her body. Not to mention the emotional strain of endless exhaustion and wrestling with piercing pain. It was torture on purpose. And that just made no sense whatsoever. The only exception, of course, was the end result the physicians meant to achieve. That's why you do it. That's why you suffer in the short term, so there is a life to live in the long term—physical and emotional scars and all.

One of the most poignant and moving illustrations of love appeared through my brother-in-law, David. It began with a phone call from a three hour time difference—West Coast to the East Coast.

"Hey brother," His voice was upbeat and cheery. "How are you doing?"

"David! Hey, good to hear your voice!" I replied.

"How's my sister doing?" He suddenly changed the mood with his concern.

"She's fighting hard. The chemo has taken the wind out of her sails, but her fight within is intense," I answered as any hurting husband would.

"Listen. Don't tell her I called. I want to surprise her," He sounded like a kid planning an attack on a menacing pirate ship. "I want to fly out to see her."

"Oh, yeah?! That would be wonderful!" I shared in his enthusiasm thinking his visit would be somewhere in the coming weeks. "When do you plan on coming out?"

"Tuesday," He blurted out. "I need your help to pick me up from the airport around 5 PM."

"What?!" I was surprised at how soon his arrival was and so pleased for Paula. "Absolutely, brother. I'll definitely be there to grab you. She's going to love seeing you and it will lift her spirits."

The Hope Parade

After our conversation, I kept my secret. As much as I wanted to tell my sweet suffering wife that her brother was going to drop in within a couple of days to see her, I held that one close to my chest. Aside from her hours of dual "cocktail" chemotherapy infusions (as if one medication was not at all worse enough), she would either rest in bed or sit comfortably on our living room sofa. We kept the interior temperature comfortable and balmy because it was winter in Pittsburgh, but she always wore a beanie to keep her bare head extra warm. The soothing glow of the blazing fireplace just a mere five feet away didn't hurt either.

When she was not asleep, she read and she talked with God about everything. She exchanged words and sometimes groans in her spirit with her Maker. Because she knew who He was in her life; she completely and unmistakably held her confidence in His will for her life. There was no way she would be angry with Him for this. Instead, she uttered sweet praises of worship and adoration to Him. Unless you encounter this relationship for yourself, it can be difficult to imagine. There was perfect peace and joy underneath her pale skin and sunken in eyes. It was given to her each day by the Prince of Peace himself.

Tuesday had arrived just like the calendar had promised. I made sure that I left the office early to drive across town and pick up David from the Pittsburgh International Airport. I found him at curbside once his plane landed and we started our drive back to our place. It sure was great to see him. And what a surprise it was going to be.

During our hour-long commute, I brought him up to speed on every single detail concerning Paula's situation. He was deeply moved and saddened. During times like this, we really missed our family members. Living across the country for Noah's medical needs isolated us from those whom we cherished. Having David in my car was proof that my heart jumped for joy because of his presence.

We parked in front of our townhome and he wasted no time jumping out of the passenger seat. Clearly, he was on a mission. On the way home, we agreed that I would open the door, walk in first, and he would casually follow me through the living room several steps behind. And that's how it played out.

Roger R. Ziegler

"Hi baby," I greeted Paula as she sat in her favorite part of the sofa. As I leaned over her to kiss her, my body concealed her brother behind me. As I stood back up, her eyes shifted away from my face over to a familiar figure that stood in our living room.

"Hi sis," David said wearing the biggest smile you can find anywhere. He walked towards her as she realized this was really happening to her.

"David!" She called out with every bit of strength she could muster. "You're here!" Her voice was strained and we could hear the weakness in her body through her words. But her countenance lit up the better part of the state. It was priceless.

David gently hugged her tired frame and kissed her on her cheek. She couldn't contain her tears and he joined in some too. He sat right next to her and removed his Army green beanie to reveal a clean, nearly shaved head. Paula noticed his bald head and knew why he cut off his hair. It was a love statement in support of his little sister. Because love does something.

I can tell you the next couple of hours I witnessed a lift and a boost in Paula. Sure, her exhausted frame may have tried to cover her sheer happiness and gratitude for her brother's unexpected arrival, but I could see it for miles. She was dancing on the inside and it was evident to me.

And just like that, David was like the wind. He had to return to work and took an early AM flight home the next day. It was an act of brotherly love and it was his best impression of exactly who he was—a brother devoted to his sister and if he could somehow eliminate her suffering by trading places, he would do so without hesitation.

Hope is sent sometimes in unannounced visits, like overnight delivery packages left on our doorstep by people driving big brown trucks. David couldn't spend more time with his sister during her most daunting battle, but he did the unthinkable and most wonderful thing anyone could do—visit his sister during the most arduous moments of her physical state of health.

In her time spent conversing with Jesus, she thanked him for sending David with his terrific smile. She also asked for blessings in a variety of shapes and sizes, colors and patterns. Jesus never disappoints. In fact, his love for us is so remarkable that we have a difficult time comprehending it fully. God heard every word and collected every one of her tears. He wasn't delighted in her suffering either. But He allowed it to happen for His plan to weave through the fabric of her life on this earth. Jesus was right there every minute of every day, right by her side. And when He knew she needed a hopeful lift, He sent David to her side. At just the right time from across our vast country.

~

Her treatment phase of chemotherapy ended in May. It was six long and stressful months. After further testing was performed to monitor and evaluate her cancer, it was determined that the chemo was not effective in the reduction of the tumor size. However, a large percentage of the cells in and around the mass was terminated. Mission accomplished.

The next phase of treatment was surgery. A surgeon removed her left breast and also created a new one from her belly area. They call it a reconstructive flap procedure. They also removed 13 lymph nodes from her left armpit region and one from her sternum (breast bone). It was a radical surgical procedure and would require a lengthy recovery.

When the physicians examined the extracted lymph nodes they found clusters of thriving cancer cells, making the timing of such surgery very crucial. But the evidence was clear—cancer had surely spread throughout her body and into other areas such as her sternum region.

Paula handled everything with grace and patience. A true warrior was in our presence and she braved this storm like a powerhouse. We all rallied around her and helped support this ongoing course of care.

Finally, once she healed from the surgery, she was treated with radiation therapy localized to her left chest region to eradicate all remaining cancer. These treatment visits were often and numbered to nearly thirty in all. Her skin began to show signs of slight burns and discoloration. It was uncomfortable at first and became painful as they continued in number.

By the end of summer, her cancer was removed and was destroyed by the surgery and radiation. We cheered and celebrated Paula's victory, to say the least. I was overjoyed with her victory. She fought for so long and with each bit of desire she had. The wigs she had purchased along the way were now no longer required because her hair grew back to cute, short lengths. She got her groove back!

We exhaled a collective sigh of relief. The beast of cancer was defeated. The following few years required two reconstructive surgeries and her transformation was complete. Or, at least as complete as the physicians had planned. Although, she continued with a preventative dose of chemo, very common to these patients, and kept a close watch for any reoccurring growth. Unfortunately, she had the type of cancer that has a very high chance of returning. But her hope isn't in the course of treatment, the clinical methods of monitoring progress, or how well her immune system can fight off any future invasions. Her hope is carefully and wholly placed in her Healer, Jesus.

As our vows were exchanged to each other almost thirty years ago in that beautiful church setting in Downey, California, little did we comprehend the weight behind such words of our promise. "In sickness and in health" became surreal on this side of my bride's cancer journey. Because there were plenty of healthy days within our many years of marriage, this heightened level of sickness she endured seemed like a towering mountain by comparison.

No matter where she was in that wide spectrum state of being, there was nothing on this side of Pluto that was ever going to make me leave her side. I guess a falling star from beyond our universe could make the attempt, but I will never give up the fight to continue and be her loving husband. Being married to her is purely sensational.

HOPE...*Renews*

When life's twists and turns wreak havoc, hope renews our strength to continue. When defeat looks imminent and our hearts are crushed–hope wins! Isaiah 40:31

My Darkest Days

They say that hope shines brighter when it lives and breathes inside of darkness. I can attest to that statement. At least it did for me. Because my darkest days were recent, suffocating, and looked like the deepest shades of empty black found at the center of an Event Horizon.

My son, Noah, lived a turbulent life right out of the womb. The most difficult portion being the life-threatening illness that nearly consumed him when he was nine and plagued the rest of his years. For a vivid picture of his earlier years through grade school, you can read my memoir titled: *Patchwork Kid: A Boy's Transplant Journey of Hope through the Midst of Tragedy*.

In 2017, we witnessed a sharp decline in his overall health that required him to return home for aggressive treatment of liver rejection. Not what a 23-year-old person desires after experiencing almost a year in another state filled with glorious sunshine and the Rocky Mountains of Colorado.

You see, in 2004, he received a three-organ transplant; a liver, part of the small intestine, and a pancreas. These precious organs gave him the gift of life as he clung to every one of his days that led up to that timely surgery. He spent the next three years in a health crisis and it demanded we move our family from our home in Southern California to Pittsburgh, PA to be near the surgeons that saved him in 2004. So, in 2008, we made our trek across the country to keep him alive.

It seemed that he fought numerous ongoing health threats that included liver rejection episodes at least once every year. The transplant team did everything within their expertise to reverse the rejections and save his organ. It was God's hand and favor on our son.

Enter 2017. After a phone call with Noah who was at his home in Colorado, it was revealed to us how sick he had become. Years upon years of frustration, battle weariness, desperation, and disappointment caused him to suffer quietly and somewhat ignore what he was certain about. I can't begin to define and uncover every single one of his emotions through years of trauma, but I plan on doing so in my sequel to *Patchwork Kid*. Just take my word for it that his emotional state was wounded by nuclear-sized blasts all throughout his childhood, adolescent years, and the years that followed. He was tired. He wanted to revert to that kid before life was utter chaos and pull the covers over his eyes as if the monster was not in his room. But life doesn't work like that.

Upon his return home to Pittsburgh, we rallied around our son in support of his battle against this unforgiving illness. Months took their toll on him, on his siblings who continued to witness his destruction through sickness, and on us as parents. Emotionally, I was slammed with the atrocities that inflicted my son. The enemy was striking our home with bolts of lightning, so to speak, and it only increased with intensity as Noah grew older. My weapons of defense were God's word and His promises throughout, intense prayer, and resting at my Lord's side while He fought on our behalf. Our hope may have looked weathered and beaten, but it never left.

By early 2018, the words of victory were delivered from the transplant team. We were elated to learn that his liver had dramatically turned for the better. It was pure joy and about a three-ton size of relief we experienced. I don't think we dodged a bullet but actually avoided being shredded with M134D Gatling machine gun fire that is delivered at over two-thousand rounds per minute. Whew!

Noah realized he had to remain with us longer than he wanted to, because of his strict course of follow up care with the team. He was able to find work and was hired by Target close to our townhouse. It was perfect and he absolutely enjoyed being back to a productive lifestyle of earning and contributing his value to the marketplace. His health had reached new heights and his strength to new levels. His thin 5'-10" frame began to pack on pounds of muscle from his truck unloading shifts at work and from exercises at home.

We found new days of joy from his presence. After seeing his journey through so much illness from birth, and from his onset of crisis at age nine through his early adulthood, we appreciated the gifts of thriving he experienced. I looked forward to waking at 5:30 AM to drive him to work on those days when I needed the car. I enjoyed having coffee with him and sharing his foodie cravings. His laugh infected the home and added to the happiness shared with our other son, Luke, and of course our Mini-Pin dog, Trixie.

And then life happens. I know with all certainty that lightning does strike in the same place twice. In fact, more like dozens of times.

On September 31, 2018, Noah was hospitalized again. This time it appeared that rejection didn't contain itself to only one organ, but it had invaded all three of his transplanted organs at once. The fight would be daunting and uphill at the very least.

Rounds of Thymoglobulin and other specific drugs were administered to reverse the rejection and start Noah back on his way to health. Like chemo, these drugs inflict severe punishment on his body in terrifying ways during their course of aid. Days and weeks had passed. He was still a temporary resident of the Children's Hospital of Pittsburgh and treated by their world-class transplant team.

We loved him immensely and held him through the days and nights. We cried with him and encouraged him to fight. We remained diligently with him through the toughest parts of his life, just like all of those years before. Only instead of him wearing SpongeBob pajamas as a nine-year-old, he was a young man with vibrant tattoos, piercings, enormous ear lobe gauges, and his reddish-brown facial hair. A man to the world, but he was still our boy, our oldest son.

By October, he began to suffer internal hemorrhaging within his intestine. By November, his weakened and frail body showed signs of unmistakable calamity. We had every ounce of belief our son would recover, even at the slowest pace, up until early December. His third surgery attempt to stop the waves of internal hemorrhaging proved to the transplant surgeons that his body was breaking down. By this time, Noah was under an induced medical coma and my three other children, my wife, and I were no less under a different type of emotional comatose. Our lives came crashing down.

I will reserve the many details of his 10-week intense fight and the days/weeks/months that followed for another day. The accounts are all too vivid and my heart is openly raw, being that this was only seven months ago. But I choose to include this within the pages of this book to show you that no matter how ugly, painful, disastrous, or bleak the situation is, the blessed hope of Jesus will always be present.

Noah Paul Ziegler, our 25-year-old son, passed on in the intensive care unit of Children's Hospital on the evening of December 6, 2018. He changed addresses. Now face to face with his savior, Jesus, Noah was healed from a life of affliction and suffering. He was permanently made whole and present in his new home.

So now what does that mean for me, for us? Do we abandon ship and run for cover to any and everything this world has to offer for comfort? No way. Why? Because our comfort is in Jesus. He is our present help and He is our perfect hope.

Grief is a monster, at minimum. It's something you can't fend off with a large broom or chase away by banging tin garbage can lids. Grief and its friends, adversity, and despair, have camped out in front of my lawn. Uninvited guests who are trespassing. And here's the strangest part: grief, in this context, is necessary for me to heal. Now that's strange and tastes worse than curdled milk. But it's true.

My beautiful wife and I say that we grieve with hope. That's what we do. Because the process is inevitable and our healing requires it. The pain is suffocating at times. I have found myself driving behind the wheel and sobbing uncontrollably. DUI—driving under the influence...of grief.

My loss is deep. My pain is severe. But I know who holds me up and I can brave each day with the comfort of knowing I will laugh with Noah again. Even when my darkest days are upon me, I am rescued by the joy of knowing who God is for me. And just like that eight-year-old boy who trusted in Jesus and became the recipient of hope with no expiration date, I remove that Everlasting Gobstopper from its wrapper and taste the goodness of God's glorious expectation. Similar to the man in the clouds who believed in his final hour and was personally assured paradise, much like when Jesse experienced *The Hope Parade* marching through his hospital room, I too have the greatest hope anyone can ever have.

HOPE... *Is Jesus*

Life is wonderful and it is filled with extreme sweetness, the discovery of amazement, and sensational heart-pounding moments. For some, those wonders occur at a frequent pace and continue moment after moment, for years upon years. And for others, those same wonders may only appear occasionally and periodically. Nevertheless, they do appear and some lives appreciate these blessings.

Otherwise, opposing events to the sweet—almost like a salty layer across a bed of dark chocolate—spread across the landscape of each one's journey mark difficult obstacles. Difficulties can take many forms and they represent a common theme: attempt to cause disruption of the goodness within life.

The fiercest calamity is no match for Jesus. Never has and never will. Yet sometimes we make our vacation plans right in the middle of our troubles and pitch our tents within arm's reach of its campfire glow. We entertain the thought of its power by fueling it with our best serving of fear. We focus every ounce of strength on it too. I know because I've been there.

Like Peter, who once walked on the surface of the water but began to sink beneath it because he put his eyes on it instead, we have a choice. Should we choose to recall over and over the fact that our feet are not designed to walk on the surface of the water here in our world, restricted by the laws of physics? That perhaps it is simply impossible to rise over the depths of overwhelming situations and the only logical outcome is our demise by sinking below.

Or, we can embrace the power freely handed over to us by Jesus himself, via a personal relationship, and remember that He transforms our thinking, mindset, and perspective to be different. We may have forgotten this. I know that I have at times in my walk with Him. I can choose to set my eyes on the things above with my Heavenly mind and realize that the storm can exist in my life, but it will not separate me from God's love. That, my friends, is true power.

Yes, I can walk within the stormy sea and even upon the surface of it because of who Jesus is. I will not drown. I will not be consumed. Unless I allow those things to be what I embrace and nurture, I will overcome. But why would I ever want to focus, feed, and listen to despair? Because I have the ability to engage with the Prince of Peace himself and adopt His truth, His peace, and His comfort during the storms. I would much rather listen to His voice and spend time with Him amidst those crashing waves.

The fiercest calamity is weak at best when it cowers beside the magnitude of our Lord. So, don't convince yourself in rendering first aid to it. Don't apply any of your concern towards it or put your focus on it. No, let calamity in your life become overshadowed by the grace of Jesus who gives you the power to be more than conquerors. Go ahead and be what He intends you to be. You are His now and find rest in His arms of mighty love.

If you don't know Jesus, introduce yourself to Him. He is waiting, He loves you and He wants to be your source of hope and so much more. And you, my friend, will never be the same.

~

The Hope Parade

And just like that, the dazzling and wonderful entrance of the Hope Parade has fulfilled its purpose. I pray for your heart to flutter with encouragement and for your days to feel the warm comfort of glorious expectations. You are going to be more than just alright; you can expect a peace that surpasses understanding to replace diabolical fear.

At last, you can easily exhale and shake the dust of adversity from your feet. Now you can face your next chapter with confidence, with assurance. Perhaps, boldly go where you never have been before. What a great concept, right?

So, I charge you with this decision...embrace hope.

Roger R. Ziegler

The Hope Parade

The Hope Parade

Made in the USA
Monee, IL
01 June 2023